Wait! WHAT?

TEDDY ROOSEVELT Was a Moose?

DAN GUTMAN

illustrated by **ALLISON STEINFELD**

NORTON YOUNG READERS

An Imprint of W. W. Norton & Company
Independent Publishers Since 1923

To kids who like to learn cool stuff.

Photograph on page 11 courtesy of National Park Service,
Manhattan Historic Sites Archive.

For information about permission to reproduce selections from this book, write to
Permissions, W. W. Norton & Company, Inc., 500 Fifth Avenue, New York, NY 10110

For information about special discounts for bulk purchases, please contact
W. W. Norton Special Sales at specialsales@wwnorton.com or 800-233-4830

Manufacturing by Sheridan
Book design by Patrick Collins
Production manager: Anna Oler

ISBN 978-1-324-01564-2
ISBN 978-1-324-01708-0 (pbk.)

W. W. Norton & Company, Inc.
500 Fifth Avenue, New York, N.Y. 10110
www.wwnorton.com

W. W. Norton & Company Ltd.
15 Carlisle Street, London W1D 3BS

2 4 6 8 0 9 7 5 3 1

CONTENTS

That's True, But…

Hi everybody. I'm Paige, and this is my little brother Turner. Do you know what's really interesting?

Yeah, kitty litter. Think about it. Somebody had to invent that stuff. Before kitty litter, how did people have indoor cats? I guess they just had stinky houses.

"Whenever you are asked if you can do a job, tell 'em, 'certainly I can!' Then get busy and find out how to do it."

Who cares about *that*? I'll tell you what's *really* interesting—famous people. I've read a bunch of biographies for kids , but they always leave out the *good* parts. The cool stuff. The *strange* things. So Turner and I decided to learn about famous people and write about them. But we leave out the boring junk and just include the good stuff.

2

Oh yeah. I guess famous people are interesting too.

Like Teddy Roosevelt, for instance. He was one of the most famous men of the twentieth century. He was one of our presidents, of course, but he was also a cowboy, a cattle rancher, an explorer, a war hero, and an environmentalist. He was the father of the United States Navy. He almost died a bunch of times. And over a hundred years later, people are still arguing about whether he was a good guy or a bad guy. We could probably fill *two* books about Teddy Roosevelt.

After this, can we do a book all about kitty litter?

No! You're impossible!

Meow.

CHAPTER 1

Stuff Your Teacher Wants You to Know About Teddy Roosevelt…

October 27, 1858 Born in New York City. The building where he was born is now a museum dedicated to him.

1880 Marries Alice Hathaway Lee.

1882 Member of the New York State Assembly. Serves in the New York Army National Guard. Writes his first book, *The Naval War of 1812*.

1884 His first child, Alice Lee Roosevelt, is born. His wife, Alice, dies two days later.

1886 Marries Edith Carow. They will have five children together.

1895 President of the New York City Board of Police Commissioners.

YAY!

1897 Assistant Secretary of the Navy.

Woo Hoo! **1899** Governor of New York.

1901 Serves as vice president. Becomes president of the United States.

1904 Wins reelection. *BOO!*

1906 Wins the Nobel Peace Prize.

1912 Runs for president again. Loses. Survives assassination attempt.

1919 Dies at the age of sixty. He is buried in Youngs Memorial Cemetery, in Oyster Bay, New York.

2001 Wins the Medal of Honor.

2020 It is announced that his statue will be removed from the front of the American Museum of Natural History.

 Still awake? Great! Okay, let's get to the good stuff, the stuff your teacher doesn't even know about Teddy Roosevelt . . .

"It is hard to fail, but it is worse never to have tried to succeed."

CHAPTER 2

Young TR

 We should probably start by getting the guy's name right. It was Theodore. Most people called him Teddy, but he hated that name. He said, "No one in my family has ever used it, and if it is used by anyone it is a sure sign that he does not know me."

His childhood nickname was Teedie. But I think it would make things simplest here if we just call him TR. Short and sweet. Agreed?

Agreed. TR it is.

His father's family was Dutch, and they were wealthy. They had immigrated to America in the 1600s and settled in New York. His father owned a plate glass company. He was one of the founders of the Metropolitan Museum of Art, the American Museum of Natural History, and the YMCA.

I love that song! His mother's family had a few bucks themselves. They owned a plantation in Georgia. It must have been like the Civil War in that house.

It was. In fact, TR's mother (who was called Mittie) supported the Confederacy during the Civil War. Her family were slaveholders. She would put together packages of medicine, clothing, and money and smuggle them to her friends in the South.

 TR had an older sister named Anna (nicknamed "Bamie"), a younger brother named Elliott ("Ellie"), and a younger sister named Corinne ("Conie"). Elliott grew up to become the father of Eleanor Roosevelt, who was the wife of President Franklin Delano Roosevelt. More on all of them later.

 Do you know how TR was related to FDR?

 Everybody knows that. They were fifth cousins.

 Oh yeah? Well, here's a cool story you don't know. When Abraham Lincoln was assassinated in 1865, TR was six years old. Lincoln's funeral

parade came to New York City. Thousands of people paid their respects. The parade went right by TR's grandfather's house on Broadway.

What's so cool about that?

This. In the 1950s, a researcher was working on a book about Lincoln when he came across this photo. It was taken that day, April 25, 1865. That's TR's grandfather's house across the street.

So?

Look in the second-story window between the shutters. There are two figures there. Do you know who they are?

Batman and Robin?

Funny. The two figures are TR and his brother Elliott watching the funeral.

How do you know that?

TR's childhood friend Edith Carow was there that day. When she was very old, she was shown the photo and she identified them. She said, "They didn't like my crying. They took me and locked me in a back room. I never did see Lincoln's funeral."

Wow!

Mind and Body

TR was sick a lot as a kid. He had severe asthma. Do you know how they treated asthma in those days?

Let me guess. With lots of rest and fresh air?

No. With black coffee and tobacco!

Wait! What? Get outta here!

No kidding. That was a *thing*! They gave people coffee and tobacco like it was medicine! Even kids!

Wow. It's amazing that TR survived to become an adult.

He also had really bad eyesight. When he finally got his first pair of glasses, he said, "I had no idea how beautiful the world was."

One summer, TR went away to a camp in Maine. The other boys made fun of him for being skinny and wearing thick glasses.

Kids can be jerks.

One day, TR's father sat down with him and the two of them had a serious talk.

About the birds and the bees?

Not *that* talk! It was about the mind and the body. His father told TR, "You have the mind, but not the body, and without the help of the body the mind cannot go as far as it should."

It was a turning point in TR's life. He made it

his mission to get healthy and strong. A private gym was installed in the house. TR started taking boxing lessons. And slowly but surely, he grew up to become a big, strong man.

Dead Animals

One day, young TR was at a local market when he saw somebody selling dead seals.

Wait. What? Who sells dead seals?

I don't know. Trust me, it happened. I looked it up. Anyway, TR brought a seal home.

His parents must have freaked *out*.

Actually, they didn't. Remember, TR's father was one of the founders of the American Museum of Natural History. He encouraged TR and even hired a professional to give him lessons in taxidermy. That's the art of stuffing and mounting the skins of animals.

I know what taxidermy is!

Okay, okay! So anyway, TR created a little "Roosevelt Museum of Natural History" in his house. That was the beginning of his lifelong interest in animals and nature. He could look at the skull of an animal and tell you the exact species. When TR was just nine, he wrote a paper with the title "The Natural History of Insects."

FLY

DRAGONFLY

BUMBLEBEE

People who came over to his house never knew what they might see. There could be a tortoise or a snake in the water pitcher. Or TR might take off his hat and a bunch of frogs would jump out. One day the housekeeper found a dead mouse in the icebox.

RIBBIT

RIBBIT

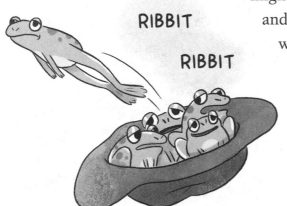

What's an icebox?

That's like a refrigerator, before they had refrigerators.

Smarty-Pants

TR was homeschooled, and he was really smart. During family trips to Europe, he learned to speak French and German. Later, he picked up Latin, Greek, and Portuguese.

He worked really hard too. He got into Harvard and decided he was going to become a scientist. He took nine classes in a semester.

That's a ridiculous number of classes.

Not only that, but at the same time he worked on the college magazine, he was vice president of the Natural History Society, and he boxed, wrestled, and rowed.

All at the same time? I can see boxing and wrestling, but it's really hard to row while you're fighting with somebody.

Very funny.

One year at college, TR met a young woman named Alice Hathaway Lee. The moment he saw her, he told a friend, "See that girl? I am going to marry her."

That's so romantic!

So he asked her to marry him, and she said no.

Oh. Not so romantic.

But TR didn't give up. He was so in love with Alice that he would wander around the woods near Harvard at night, hoping to see her. Some nights he wouldn't sleep. If another boy seemed interested in Alice, TR would challenge him to a duel. He even ordered a pair of French dueling pistols in case he needed them.

Finally, Alice changed her mind. They got married on TR's twenty-second birthday. Alice was nineteen. He called her "darling little sunshine" and she called him "Teddykins."

That's romantic!

Just before his college graduation, TR went for a medical checkup. The doctor noticed that he had an irregular heartbeat and advised him to avoid any kind of strenuous exercise, even running up stairs. Well, TR wasn't having it.

"I am going to do all the things you tell me not to do," he told the doctor. "If I've got to live the sort of life you have described, I don't care how short it is."

TR set out to prove how tough he was. On his honeymoon with Alice he climbed the Matterhorn, one of the highest mountains in Europe. Later he went on a six-week hunting trip out West.

It didn't go well. His asthma returned. He was bitten by a snake. He fell out of a wagon and landed on his head.

It must have been a confusing time for TR. He decided that he didn't want to be a scientist after all. He enrolled in law school at Columbia University, but he didn't like it and dropped out after a year. He didn't know what to do with his life.

Oooh, end the chapter with a cliff-hanger! Nice touch. It makes the reader want to know what happens next.

"Bodily vigor is good, and vigor of intellect is even better, but far above both is character."

CHAPTER 3

Tragedy and Triumph

One of the best weeks of TR's life was also one of the worst weeks of his life.

Explain.

On February 12, 1884, his wife Alice gave birth. They named the baby girl Alice Lee. TR was away when the baby was born. He rushed home, only to find out that his twenty-two-year-old wife had a serious kidney problem called Bright's disease. Not only that, but it was discovered that his mother was dying of typhoid.

🙂 Oh man.

😀 Within eleven hours, both women died. It was Valentine's Day. TR drew a big *X* in his diary for that day and wrote, "The light has gone out of my life."

Baby Lee

TR was so shaken up by what happened that for the rest of his life, he never mentioned his wife Alice again. Photos of her were removed from his scrapbooks. Her letters were destroyed. He couldn't even bring himself to say her name. Instead of calling the baby "Alice Lee," he called her "Baby Lee." Later, when TR wrote his autobiography, he didn't even mention his wife Alice once.

Tough Guy

Guess what TR did right after his wife and his mother died.

He bought four hundred cows.

How did you know that?

I did my research! TR was a wealthy New York gentleman. He could have used his family name and gotten some cushy job or run for political office. But *nooooooooo*. He decided to move to North Dakota, start a cattle ranch, and hunt buffalo.

Wait, didn't he have a new baby to take care of?

Yeah. His sister Bamie took care of Baby Lee while TR went off on his Badlands adventure. North Dakota was still the "Wild West" in those days. It was like a different world for TR, and he loved the rugged life. He learned how to rope, ride, and hunt. The exercise was good for his health. He became an even stronger man.

Instead of hanging out with a bunch of lawyers and doctors, TR was hanging out with cowboys and gamblers. He worked hard and won their respect. He even served as deputy sheriff. He also wrote three books about the people and animals he encountered living the frontier life.

One day, TR's boat was stolen from his ranch. As deputy sheriff, he decided to bring the thieves to justice. So TR and two of his ranch hands chased them for three days through freezing winter weather. Finally they captured the boat robbers. TR was going to tie them up, but he was afraid that the ropes might cut off their circulation. So guess what he did instead.

He handcuffed them to the boat?

No. He took away their boots.

Why?

It was cactus country, and he figured they wouldn't make a run for it barefoot.

Smart!

Another time, TR was relaxing in a hotel bar in Montana. Some drunk started cursing and waving guns around. The guy was out of control. He shot a bullet at the clock on the wall. Then he saw TR sitting there and called him "four eyes" because he was wearing glasses.

TR tried to ignore the drunk, but the guy ordered him to buy drinks for everyone in the bar. TR stood up and said, "Well, if I've got to, I've got to." In his autobiography, he wrote what happened next . . .

I struck quick and hard with my right just to one side of the point of his jaw, hitting with my left as I straightened out, and then again with my right. He fired the guns, but I do not know whether this was merely a convulsive action of his hands, or whether he was trying to shoot at me. When he went down he struck the corner of the bar with his head...if he had moved I was about to drop on my knees; but he was senseless. I took away his guns, and the other people in the room, who were now loud in their denunciation of him, hustled him out.

I guess he showed that guy who was boss!

The next morning, TR put the drunk on a freight train out of town.

Edith

Remember TR's childhood friend Edith Carow, the girl he locked in a closet because she was crying during Abraham Lincoln's funeral?

Yeah, what about her?

TR fell in love with her.

Wait! What? How did you know that?

I do my research *too*. Actually, TR had fallen in love with Edith one summer back in his college days, before he met his wife Alice. He asked Edith to marry him then, and she said no. And when TR married Alice, Edith Carow was at the wedding.

Awkward!

In September 1885, TR came back to New York from the Badlands and bumped into Edith again. This time they fell in love with each other and got married in London a year later.

 I'm not going to say how romantic that was.

Edith was very different from Alice. She was serious, literary, and she had a temper. She was a city girl, and she didn't want to move to North Dakota and be a rancher's wife. So they settled in New York.

What about the cattle ranch in North Dakota?

While TR was in New York, a blizzard wiped out his cattle and the ranch.

Bummer. And what happened to the baby, Alice Lee?

TR's sister Bamie had been taking care of her. But Edith didn't think that was right, so she and TR took Alice Lee in and began to build their family. But let's save that for later. We need to talk about . . .

Politics and Stuff

For a while, TR had been thinking about entering politics. But you don't just wake up one morning and run for president of the United States. Well, some people do. But most politicians start small.

So TR joined the Republican Party, ran for New York State Assembly, and won. He saw a lot of poverty and stood up to big business to improve the working conditions of women and children.

He was making a name for himself, and a lot of people said he should run for mayor of New York City. He did. But he lost.

In 1895, TR was appointed New York City police commissioner. He made it his mission to root out police corruption. After his workday was done, he would go out in the middle of the night and sneak around the streets with a hat pulled over his eyes so he wouldn't be recognized. When he found a cop breaking the rules or asleep on the job, he would discipline him.

Gotcha!

Huh?

TR's midnight adventures got written up in the newspapers, and New York policemen started looking over their shoulders for a guy in a dark cloak with blinding white teeth. Street vendors started selling whistles shaped like "Teddy's Teeth," and pranksters blew them at cops who didn't do their job.

In six short years, TR would go from sneaking around busting cops to becoming the president of the United States. But during that time, something amazing happened that made him world-famous.

Do tell!

The Rough Riders

To tell this story, we have to go back a few years. One day during his senior year at Harvard, TR was in the library. He was leafing through books about the Navy. He didn't think the books were very good, so you know what he did?

He bought four hundred more cows?

No. He decided to write his *own* book about the Navy. He started writing *The Naval War of 1812* while he was a college student, and finished it after he graduated. He was just twenty-three. The Navy was so impressed, they put a copy of the book on every ship and used it as a textbook at the Naval War College. Even today, it's the standard book on the subject.

I'm impressed!

So was President William McKinley. In 1897 he named TR Assistant Secretary of the Navy. It was an important job. America wanted to be a world power. That meant building battleships, annexing Hawaii, creating the Panama Canal, and taking control of the Caribbean. There was just one problem—Spain was dominating the Caribbean at the time.

So what did TR do?

Nothing. On February 15, 1898, the battleship USS *Maine* was docked in Havana Harbor when it suddenly exploded. Three-quarters of the crew died. To this day, nobody knows for sure what caused the explosion. But newspapers like the *World* blamed Spain and got the American public all riled up, and the next thing anybody knew, the Spanish-American War had broken out.

So you might say the blame for *Maine* fell mainly on Spain.

Very funny.

So how did TR get involved?

Well, at that point, he was about to turn forty. He could barely see without glasses. And he had six kids at home. So guess what he did.

He bought four hundred more cows?

No. He enlisted in the Army! He was named lieutenant colonel of the First United States Volunteer Cavalry. TR recruited a bunch of tough guys with no military experience to serve under him—football players, polo players, cowboys. They had nicknames like "Tough Ike," "the Dude," and "Pork Chop." As a group, they called themselves the Rough Riders.

It sounds like a good name for an action movie.

It was! In 1997, there was a TV miniseries called *Rough Riders* starring Tom Berenger as TR. Anyway, TR resigned from the Navy, packed twelve pairs of eyeglasses, and went to go fight the Spanish in Cuba. A week later, the Rough Riders became famous for their brave charge up San Juan Hill. They got credit for driving off the Spaniards. TR called it "the great day of my life."

" Don't hit a man at all if you can avoid it, but if you have to hit him, knock him out. "

A hundred and three years later, he was awarded the Medal of Honor.

A lot of good it did him then. He was dead.

But when he came back from Cuba, he was a war hero. He was greeted by cheering crowds wherever he went. People were starting to talk about "the Colonel" as a future president of the United States.

Reporters followed him everywhere. One day a reporter asked TR's son Archie where the Colonel was. "I don't know where the Colonel is," Archie replied, "but Father is taking a bath."

So TR ran for president after that?

No. He ran for governor of New York State. And he won by promising a "Square Deal" for the people—honesty, sharing, and caring. But that job didn't last very long.

How come?

The vice president, Garret A. Hobart, died.

So?

The 1900 presidential election was heating up and President McKinley needed a vice president. TR didn't want the job, but just about everyone in the Republican Party wanted him. At the national convention, TR was nominated with every vote except one—his own. McKinley won the election, and suddenly TR was the vice president of the United States. But that job didn't last long either. Just six months.

I know what happened.

Shhhh! Let's tell 'em in the next chapter! Another cliff-hanger!

CHAPTER 4

The President

On September 6, 1901, President McKinley was at an event in Buffalo, New York, when a guy suddenly walked up to him, pulled out a gun, and shot him twice in the chest. Amazingly, it looked like McKinley was going to survive. In fact, TR was so confident the president would pull through that he went on a hiking vacation.

So TR was out on a trail a few days later, taking a break for lunch. He was about to bite into his sandwich when he saw a guide coming up the trail. He wrote, "When I saw the runner, I instinctively knew he had bad news—the worst news in the world."

President McKinley was dead. TR would be the twenty-sixth president of the United States. He had become vice president when the vice president died, and he became president when the president died. He was just forty-two, and he was the youngest president in American history.

The second youngest was John F. Kennedy. He was forty-three.

By the way, when TR was sworn in, he didn't put his hand on the Bible like most presidents do. He was at a friend's house, and they couldn't find one!

Three other presidents were sworn in without a Bible—John Quincy Adams and Franklin Pierce used law books. Lyndon Johnson used a book of prayers.

Betcha didn't know this—TR's first day in the White House was his father's birthday.

Bet *you* didn't know *this*—TR didn't have a vice president for his entire first term in office.

TR wasn't like any other president before him. Suddenly the White House was filled with overnight guests—authors, sculptors, poets, artists, and boxers. It was like a three-ring circus. He was a celebrity, and he loved attention. It was said that TR "wanted to be the bride at every wedding and the corpse at every funeral."

TR invented the presidential press conference. One day it was pouring rain, and he saw a bunch of reporters huddled outside the White House. TR decided to give them their own room inside. So naturally they wrote nice things about him.

There was no radio, TV, or internet back then, so the newspaper was the only way to get the news.

42

Right. And every day at one o'clock, reporters would gather at the White House for a press conference. Often TR would be getting a shave from a barber. With shaving cream all over his face, TR would jump off the chair to answer a reporter's question, waving his arms around the whole time. Then he'd sit back in the chair. The press loved it.

I wonder how the barber felt.

The Kids

The White House was even crazier because for the first time in a long time, there were young kids running around. TR and Edith had five of them—Theodore Roosevelt Jr., Kermit, Ethel, Archibald, and Quentin. They could have formed their own basketball team.

Imagine the president of the United States chasing a bunch of kids around the White House, playing hide-and-go-seek, giving them piggyback rides, and having pillow fights.

Important government officials would be at the
White House and suddenly one of the Roosevelt
kids would roller-skate into the room or walk
around on stilts. The kids would slide down the
staircase on metal trays or pop out of giant vases
in the East Room. When they were bored, the
kids would drop water balloons on the Secret
Service agents.

TR called his kids "the bunnies." He would take
them on overnights in the woods, where he

would tell them ghost stories around a campfire and end with a bloodcurdling scream.

Do you know how TR taught his niece Eleanor to swim? He just told her to jump off the dock.

Sometimes TR would be in the middle of an important meeting when the kids would knock on the door. The meeting would have to come to an end because TR had promised to play with them. The South Lawn of the White House was turned into a baseball field.

He once wrote, "I don't think any family has enjoyed the White House more than we have."

Alice

To make things even crazier, suddenly there was a *teenager* in the White House. Remember Alice, TR's daughter from his first marriage? She was seventeen when her dad became president. Back in those days, young ladies were expected to be shy and quiet. Not Alice! She flirted with men, smoked cigarettes, bet at the racetrack, and was caught speeding by the police in her red sports car. She also went around with a pet snake named "Emily Spinach" on her neck.

She's friendly.

What a kook!

Naturally, the newspapers ate this stuff up. They called her "Princess Alice" and made her nearly as famous as the president. Every day there were stories about where Alice went, what Alice said, and what Alice wore. People named their babies after her. She was so famous that people called her "the other Washington Monument."

Alice had blue eyes and was known to wear that color, so for a while there was a fashion rage known as "Alice blue."

When Alice got married in 1906, thousands

of people lined the streets outside the White House. She married a congressman named Nicholas Longworth. He wasn't exactly boring either. He was famous for being able to play the violin behind his back or with the bow between his knees.

At one point, somebody suggested to TR that he should try controlling Alice. He replied, "I can be president, or I can attend to Alice."

Animals in the White House

TR's kids weren't the only wild animals running around the White House. There were also *real* wild animals! Besides having six dogs, TR and his family had rabbits, snakes, flying squirrels, chickens, bears, a lion, a zebra, a raccoon, a hyena, a barn owl, five guinea pigs, and a one-legged rooster. The White House might as well have been a zoo.

One time, TR's son Quentin took his pony Algonquin upstairs in the White House elevator.

They also had a parrot named Loretta that was trained to say, "Hurrah for Roosevelt."

TEN MORE ANIMALS AT TR'S WHITE HOUSE

Bill the lizard

Maude the pig

Josiah the badger

Nibble the mouse

Eli Yale the blue macaw

Baron Spreckle the hen

Peter the rabbit

Jonathan Edwards the bear

Jocko Root the horse

Sailor Boy the Chesapeake Bay retriever

Oh, One More Animal

Speaking of animals, did you know that teddy bears were named after Teddy Roosevelt?

Of course. Everybody knows that.

But everybody doesn't know the story. TR was on a bear hunt with some other hunters in 1902. The only problem was that they hunted for three days without finding any bears. Finally, a sad-looking old bear was found wandering around.

The other hunters chased it, roped it, and brought it back so TR could shoot it. But TR took one look at the little bear and said it wouldn't be sportsmanlike to kill it. He said, "I've hunted game all over America and I'm proud to be a hunter. But I couldn't be proud of myself if I shot an old, tired, worn-out bear that was tied to a tree."

That would have been the end of the story. But a cartoonist named Clifford K. Berryman drew a cartoon of the incident, and it was published in newspapers. The cartoon was spotted by Rose and Morris Michtom, a married couple who owned a candy store in Brooklyn, New York. They decided to make a stuffed bear and name it "Teddy's Bear."

The Michtoms wrote a letter to TR asking for permission. TR didn't think much of the idea, but he said okay. You can imagine what happened after that. Teddy bears became a huge fad. *Millions* of them were sold, and kids are still hugging them today.

Betcha didn't know this: Rose and Morris Michtom started the Ideal Toy Company. The company would also make Rubik's Cube and Betsy Wetsy, a doll that could drink water and then pee.

Reader and Writer

Remember the book TR wrote about the Navy when he was in college? He went on to write over thirty-five other books, before, during, and after his presidency. TR never stopped working. His idea of rest and relaxation was to write a book.

A FEW OF TR'S BOOKS

Hunting Trips of a Ranchman

The Winning of the West

The Rough Riders

The Strenuous Life

History of New York City

Hero Tales from American History

The Man with the Muck Rake

African Game Trails

Outdoor Pastimes of an American Hunter

Good Hunting

Life-Histories of African Game Animals

America and the World War

Remember, there were no computers in TR's day. There were typewriters, but mostly TR did his writing by hand.
He would dip his pen into an inkwell that was made of a rhino's foot.

TR loved to read. He would go through a book a day, and sometimes more. He always kept a book near the front door so he would have something to read while he was waiting for guests to arrive.

He also read a lot of magazines. He had a strange habit. After reading each page of a magazine, he would rip it out and throw it to the floor.

That's odd. It was said that TR had a photographic memory. He could recite poetry decades after reading it.

TR also wrote tons of letters, about 150,000 in his lifetime.

Toward the end of his life, TR wrote his autobiography. Do you know what it's called?

An Autobiography?

No. It was called *Why I Bought Four Hundred Cows.*

Wait! What?

I'm kidding. You were right. It was called *An Autobiography*. How did you know?

It was a lucky guess.

But here's the strange part. He told his whole life story, but he never mentioned his first wife or his brother Elliott. Their stories were too painful for him. But we'll get to Elliott later.

Obviously, TR cared a lot about reading and writing. He cared so much, he even tried to change the English language.

 When you think about it, English *is* a weird language. Teachers always tell you to "sound it out," but a lot of word spellings just don't make any sense. Like the word *tough*. Why is it spelled *T-O-U-G-H*? Wouldn't it be easier for everybody if it was spelled *T-U-F-F*?

Much better!

TOUGH
TUFF

Yes! So in 1906, TR joined something called the "simplified spelling movement." He announced that the Government Printing Office would change the spelling of three hundred words. Axe would become ax. Killed would become kilt. Through would become thro. Drooped would become droopt.

Something tells me that idea didn't work out.

You're right. There was a big outcry. Congress voted against spending the money to print documents with the new spellings, and TR backed off.

Manly Man

I talked about how TR was a sickly boy who got teased for wearing glasses. When he was growing up, being seen as tough or "manly" was really important to him. He liked to play tennis, but refused to be photographed playing because he didn't think it was a manly sport.

Boxing was TR's game. He loved to box, until one day he was sparring with a military aide who socked TR in the left eye. He had a detached retina and had no sight in that eye for the rest of his life. So he switched to judo.

During one formal lunch, TR and the Swiss minister started talking about judo. To demonstrate his point, TR grabbed the Swiss minister and threw him on the floor.

Cool. Hey, Paige. Do you think football is dangerous?

Sure. Is this another one of those things, like kitty litter, that has nothing to do with TR?

No, I'm getting there, believe me. If you think football is dangerous *now*, it was even more dangerous a century ago. Between 1900 and 1905, forty-five players died playing football.

No way!

Way! Guys were getting broken necks, broken backs. And there was no NFL back then. I'm talking about college students.

So what does that have to do with TR?

Be patient. Some colleges stopped their

football programs. People said the game should be banned. Anyway, TR was a big fan. He said, "I believe in rough games and in rough, manly sports. I do not feel any particular sympathy for the person who gets battered about a good deal so long as it is not fatal."

So what did he do?

He brought a bunch of coaches and football experts from Yale, Harvard, and other schools to Washington to talk about how they could make the game safer. They decided to change some of the rules. Like, they made passing legal.

Wait! What? Are you telling me that before that, quarterbacks weren't allowed to pass the ball?

That's right. And before that, a team only had to go five yards for a first down. So it was just a game of brute strength, and big pileups. They changed it to ten yards for a first down. The rule changes opened up the game, spread the players across the field more, and made it safer.

Football is still pretty dangerous.

Yeah, but not nearly as dangerous as it used to be. And TR gets a lot of credit for that.

Big Stick

TR's most famous quote was "Speak softly and carry a big stick; you will go far."

What does that mean?

Well, basically it means that you shouldn't show anger or threaten your opponents, but make them aware you'll use force if you have to. That's what TR tried to do. In 1907, he was concerned that Japan was a threat to the United States. So he ordered the Navy to move all its battleships from the Atlantic Ocean to the Pacific Ocean. It showed the world the power of the United States military without going to war.

TR said that "Speak softly and carry a big stick" was a West African proverb, but nobody knows who first said it.

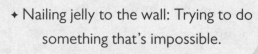

EIGHT OTHER PHRASES MADE POPULAR BY TR...

✦ Nailing jelly to the wall: Trying to do something that's impossible.

✦ Weasel words: Weak, meaningless language.

✦ Square Deal: A fair arrangement.

✦ Mollycoddle: Acting weak or cowardly.

✦ Pussyfoot: Being too cautious.

✦ Muckraker: A journalist who investigated corruption.

✦ Throw your hat in the ring: To enter a contest, like running for office. It comes from boxing.

✦ Bully pulpit: A position of authority (like being president), where your voice will be heard.

I'm actually a risk taker.

Before TR, the house where the president lived was called the "executive mansion" or the "United States Presidential Mansion." But starting in 1901, official stationery was engraved with the words "The White House."

Being president of the United States is a really hard job, and it's good to get out of Washington once in a while to relax. At one point, Edith bought a cabin in the woods of Virginia. They named it Pine Knot. She knew TR would be annoyed if Secret Service agents were hanging around the cabin, but she wanted to be safe. So Edith secretly arranged for two agents to hide in a nearby farmhouse during the day and then stand guard outside the cabin at nine o'clock each night. She never told TR.

TR hated his official presidential portrait, which was painted by an artist named Théobald Chartran. His family said it made him look like a "mewing cat." One of his last acts as president was to have the painting burned. John Singer Sargent was hired to make another one, and TR liked that one much better.

If you happened to be walking along the banks of the Potomac River in 1903, you might have seen a strange sight—the president of the United States swimming, totally naked. TR did that frequently, even during the winter.

One time, he was taking a walk with the French ambassador and the head of the United States Forest Service when the three of them decided to take a dip in the river. They stripped down, except the French ambassador kept his gloves on. When TR asked him why he was keeping his gloves on, the ambassador said, "We might meet ladies."

Just an FYI: other presidents who liked to skinny-dip—John Quincy Adams, Andrew Jackson, and John F. Kennedy.

"Knowing what's right doesn't mean much unless you do what's right."

CHAPTER 5
Accomplishments

TR's years in the White House weren't just a bunch of pillow fights and skinny-dips. He got a lot done. When historians rank the best presidents in history, TR usually finishes in the top five. When it came time to deciding which presidents should be on Mount Rushmore, TR was chosen to be next to George Washington, Abraham Lincoln, and Thomas Jefferson. Here are just a few of the things he got done as president . . .

Trust Buster

In TR's time, some companies had become so big and powerful, they could drive their competition out of business and charge unfair prices for their products. They were called "trusts." Even though TR was born rich, he fought to regulate and break up these companies to make business fairer for ordinary people. He filed forty-four antitrust lawsuits, and he was called a "trust buster."

The Panama Canal

In the old days, to go from New York to California, ships had to travel all the way around the bottom of South America. Look at it on the map. That's crazy! So TR convinced Congress to approve a canal that would be built across fifty miles of Panama. It cut the length of the trip in half. TR said the Panama Canal was one of the most important accomplishments of his presidency.

TR took a trip down to Panama in 1906 to watch the progress of the canal being built. He even got to try out a steam shovel. That was the first time a United States president traveled outside the country while he was in office.

Do You Want Rat Dung with Your Burger?

In 1904, the author Upton Sinclair spent seven weeks working in the meatpacking plants of Chicago. He found they were totally disgusting. They used old, diseased cattle. Sausage had rats and rat dung in it.

Gross!

Here's the worst part. You better sit down for this one. There were times when workers fell into vats of meat and *died* in there! The bodies were processed into meat products.

 Wait! What? No!

 It's true! Sinclair wrote a novel called *The Jungle* that described the way beef and pork were processed and packed in the United States. Everybody freaked out, of course. In 1906, TR pushed Congress to pass the Meat Inspection Act and the Pure Food and Drug Act.

 Wait, Congress had to be *pushed* to do that?

 Apparently. After that, our food was more carefully inspected and labels were put on food to tell people exactly what was in it.

The Nobel Prize

Did you ever hear of the Russo-Japanese War?

No. Does "Russo" mean Russian?

Yeah. In 1904 and 1905, over 130,000 soldiers died as Russia and Japan fought over territory. TR brought both sides together in Portsmouth, New Hampshire, to work out their differences. For that, he became the first American to win the Nobel Peace Prize.

Conservation

Ever since he was a kid, TR was fascinated by animals. Of all the presidents, TR was the pioneer who was first known for protecting them and the environment. When he was president, the United States Forest Service and five new national parks were established. He saved Yellowstone National Park from developers. The Grand Canyon, Niagara Falls, and sixteen other sites became protected national monuments. Millions of acres of land were placed under public protection.

Hey, did you know that women's hats used to be decorated with bird feathers?

No, but what does that have to do with TR?

You'll see. A hundred years ago, hunters were killing millions of exotic birds to get feathers for those silly hats. Some animal species were going extinct. So in 1903, TR signed an executive order to make a federal bird reserve at Pelican Island, Florida. It was the first time the government put land aside for wildlife. By the time his presidency was over, he had created fifty-one bird refuges all over the country.

CHAPTER 6

After the Presidency

Most presidents fade away into a quiet retirement. You don't hear much about them after they leave office. Not *this* guy.

One of the first things TR did after his term ended in 1909 was to go on a big-game hunting safari in Africa. TR returned home to New York and found he was still as popular as when he left. Huge crowds lined Broadway to greet him. He was so popular, a lot of people begged

him to run for president in 1912. "Roosevelt for President" clubs were formed all over the country. TR said no at first, but then he changed his mind and decided to run for a third term.

The only problem was that both of the major political parties had already chosen their candidates. The Republicans stuck with William Howard Taft, who was president after TR. The Democrats nominated Woodrow Wilson. So do you know what TR did?

He bought four hundred more cows?

No! TR started a *third* party, the Progressive Party. It was called the Bull Moose Party after TR told reporters, "I'm as fit as a bull moose."

So is that why we titled the book *Teddy Roosevelt Was a Moose?*

That's right.

That's weak. By the way, TR and Taft had an interesting relationship. They had been friends, but when they were running for president against one another, TR said Taft was a "fathead" with "brains less than a guinea pig."

Ooooh, that's cold! Hey, this is going to blow your mind. Three weeks before the election, TR was on his way to a rally in Milwaukee when some guy suddenly stood up, pointed a gun at him, and shot him in the chest!

And, amazingly, he survived.

Yes! And this is the mind-blowing part. Ever since he lost a pair of eyeglasses as a kid, TR always carried an extra pair with him. When he got shot, the bullet ripped through his coat, pierced the steel eyeglass case in his chest pocket, and even went right through his fifty-page speech. The bullet lodged in his chest muscle just below a rib.

🧑 Wait! What? Unbelievable! He was like Superman!

👩 It gets better. The crowd grabbed the assassin. TR shouted, "Stand back! Don't hurt the man!" TR's shirt was soaked with blood. But he knew a thing or two about injuries. He coughed and put his hand to his mouth to see if any blood came out. When it didn't, he knew he wasn't going to die. Do you know where they took him after that?

🧑 To a hospital, I hope.

👧 No! He insisted on going to the rally!

🧑 Wait! What? Get out!

👩 The people at the rally didn't know TR had been shot. So he started his speech by saying,

"Friends, I shall ask you to be as quiet as possible. I don't know whether you fully understand that I have just been shot." Then he reached into his pocket and pulled out his speech with a bullet hole in the middle of it! He said, "You see it takes more than one bullet to kill a Bull Moose."

That is a great story!

It's not done. TR spent the next ninety minutes giving his speech. Finally he let the doctors examine him. They took an X-ray to find the bullet, but decided it would be too dangerous to remove it. So TR had that bullet in his chest for the rest of his life. And today, the speech and the bloody shirt he wore that day are on display at the Theodore Roosevelt Birthplace National Historic Site in New York City.

Wow! I bet after all that excitement, he won the 1912 election easily.

No, he lost! Woodrow Wilson became president. But TR did get more votes (4.1 million) than Taft (3.4 million).

You just reminded me that TR almost got killed another time. In 1902 he was riding in a carriage in Massachusetts when it got hit by a trolley car. A Secret Service agent was killed and TR was hurt badly. He had emergency surgery, and he insisted on watching as the doctor cut into his leg. He never completely recovered, but he didn't let the public know how much pain he was in.

The guy was tough. He really was like a moose!

One Last Adventure

In 1914, TR was fifty-six, and he wasn't as strong as a Bull Moose anymore. But he felt he had one more wilderness adventure in him. When he was invited to go on a trip to South America, he jumped at the chance. "I have to go," he said. "It's my last chance to be a boy!"

Oh, I know this story. The mission was to explore a river that ran through the Amazon rain forest. It had never been mapped before, and it was called the River of Doubt. TR brought his son Kermit and a team of paddlers and porters. They set out in seven wooden canoes with enough food to last fifty days.

For forty-eight days, they didn't see another other human being. They hacked their way through the jungle with machetes and waded through water up to their hips. Their boots and clothes rotted. They had fevers. Five of the canoes were destroyed going through rapids.

"We were drenched with sweat. We were torn by the spines of innumerable clusters of small pines with thorns like needles. We were bitten by the hosts of fire-ants, and by the mosquitos, which we scarcely noticed when the fire-ants were found, exactly as all dread of the latter vanished when we were menaced by the big red wasps, of which a dozen stings will disable a man."

One of the guys in the group died. Another one went insane and ran off into the jungle. TR hurt his leg again. It became infected, and he got dysentery and malaria. His temperature went up to 105 and he couldn't walk. It looked like he was going to die. *Again.*

He begged to be left behind. He thought about ending his life. But in the end he lived, and the mission was a success. They mapped out fifteen hundred miles of the river. In TR's honor, Brazil named the river Rio Roosevelt. Today, people call it Rio Teodoro.

When he got back home, TR had lost fifty-seven pounds. He would be bothered by malaria and problems with his legs for the rest of his life.

In 1917, he was fifty-eight, and he had a lot of physical ailments. But World War I was raging in Europe, and TR still wanted to fight. He volunteered to lead a military unit and go to France. Luckily, President Wilson turned him down.

The next year, TR developed rheumatism. His feet were swollen so much that he couldn't wear shoes.

TR died in his sleep on January 5, 1919. His last words were to his servant: "James, will you please put out the light?"

"This country will not be a good place for any of us to live in if it is not a reasonably good place for all of us to live in."

CHAPTER 7

What's the Problem with Teddy Roosevelt?

Well, I guess it's time for us to talk about the big question.

You mean the question about who invented kitty litter?

No, dope! We have to discuss whether TR was a good guy or a bad guy.

Wait! What? We just spent six chapters talking about what an amazing person TR was!

I know. He *was* amazing. But there's another side to him, and we should discuss it.

Okay, I guess you're right. Where do we begin?

You know that famous statue of him outside the American Museum of Natural History in New York? He was on horseback, with a Native American and an enslaved African man walking below him on either side of the horse. In 2017, people pointed out that the statue was racist and protesters threw red paint on it. After a few years of discussion and protests, it was removed from the museum.

That's just a statue. You can't blame TR for a statue that was made of him.

It's not *just* the statue. TR was opposed to civil rights for Black people. He didn't think African Americans should be allowed to vote. He kicked 167 Black soldiers out of the Army who had been wrongfully accused of murder.

Yeah, but he was also the first president to invite a Black man—Booker T. Washington—to have dinner at the White House. None

of the presidents before him had done that. And during World War I, TR tried to recruit a regiment of Black troops.

That's true, but the fact is, TR viewed non-white people as inferior to white Americans. He called Native Americans "savages." He said that Filipinos were not capable of governing themselves. If TR were alive today and he said the things he said back then, he would be considered a racist.

Yeah, but you could say that about George Washington and Thomas Jefferson too. They were *slave owners*. Even Abraham Lincoln, who freed the slaves, said stuff that would be called racist today.

You're right. I'm not arguing with you. Let's talk about TR's military career.

What about it? He was a hero. He and the Rough Riders helped win the Spanish-American War.

On the other hand, people argue that we didn't have to fight that war. The United States was never threatened by Cuba or Spain. TR and other politicians wanted America to become a global power. They wanted the United States to control the Caribbean and other parts of the world.

But TR wasn't even president yet during the Spanish-American War. He just fought in it. You can't blame him for that war. Next I suppose you're going to tell me that TR wasn't a great conservationist.

Well, now that you brought it up, remember all those national parks he started? Remember all those national monuments and millions of acres of land he set aside to be protected?

Yeah, what about them?

Who do you think lived on that land before TR's time?

Uh, the Native Americans?

Exactly. At least *some* of that land was *their* land. The United States just took it over and pushed them off the land.

🙂 Yeah, but—

😄 And remember that African safari TR went on?

🙂 What about it?

😄 He brought his son, a bunch of scientists, soldiers, and two hundred and sixty porters to carry all their stuff. They brought along a laboratory, a taxidermist shop, and four tons of salt.

🙂 They must have really liked salty food.

😄 No, dope! They brought along all that salt to preserve the animals they were going to shoot. They killed five hundred and twelve animals, including seventeen lions, eleven elephants, twenty rhinoceroses, nine giraffes, forty-seven gazelles, eight hippopotamuses, twenty-nine zebras, nine hyenas, and some bongos, dik-diks, kudus, aardwolfs, and klipspringers.

🙂 Wait. What? Back it up. I never even heard of those last five animals.

😄 Look 'em up!

🙂 But did you know that he sent them back to

the Smithsonian and the American Museum of Natural History to be put on display? That's why we have all those beautiful dioramas of animals in museums today. He killed those animals for science!

Something tells me he also just liked shooting and killing animals.

Let's agree to disagree on that one.

Okay, let's talk about women.

Are you going to tell me TR hated women?

No, but he said that women should have as many babies as possible, and he said that women who didn't have children were selfish.

Yeah, but he also said . . . wait a minute. I wrote this quote down.

Go ahead, I'll wait.

Oh, here it is. He said, "Women should have free access to every field of labor which they care to enter, and when their work is as valuable as that of a man it should be paid as highly." TR was *way* ahead of his time when it came to women's rights. I mean, in those days, women in America couldn't even vote. That didn't happen until the year after TR died.

That just proves my point, Turner! TR was a complicated man, just like George Washington, Thomas Jefferson, and Abraham Lincoln were complicated men.

Wait. Are you admitting that great men and women can have flaws?

Exactly! TR was a racist—

Except when he wasn't.

He was an animal lover—

Who loved shooting animals.

He was a war hero—

Who won the Nobel Peace Prize.

He grew up wealthy—

But he hated big businessmen and fought to improve the lives of working people.

He believed in equality for women—

But he said their job was to have lots of babies.

He was a man of action—

But he read a book a day, and he wrote thirty-eight of them.

See what I mean?

So what do *you* think?

Not everything is black or white, Turner! We'd like life to be simple, but it's not. TR did some good stuff and some not-so-good stuff. He lived in a different time. The world has changed a lot in the last hundred years.

 I agree. And I think we can leave it at that!

"The only man who never makes mistakes is the man who never does anything."

CHAPTER 8

Oh Yeah?
(Stuff About Teddy Roosevelt That Didn't Fit Anywhere Else)

TR loved to eat, and his waistline got bigger as he got older. He liked peaches and cream for breakfast. He would eat a whole chicken and drink four glasses of milk in one sitting. He drank cup after cup of coffee with seven lumps of sugar in it. And his coffee cup, according to his son, was "more in the nature of a bathtub."

Do you know what TR's guides called him during his hunting trip through Africa?

Teddy?

No.

Teedie?

No.

Mr. President?

No. They called him "Bwana Tumbo," which means "Mr. Stomach" in Swahili.

Ouch! That had to hurt.

But TR was not a drinker. He didn't like alcohol. He would have a glass of wine to be sociable, but waiters were told to fill his glass with ice to dilute it. Even so, in newspaper articles he was often accused of being a drunk.

I can see that. He had such an outrageous personality. It could have looked like he had been drinking.

TR usually ignored the criticism, but at one point he decided he'd had enough. He sued a newspaper in Michigan that had written, "Roosevelt lies and curses in a most disgusting way; he gets drunk too, and not that infrequently." At the trial, not one witness said they ever saw TR drunk. He won the lawsuit and told the judge that was good enough for him. He hadn't sued to get money. But the judge ordered the newspaper to pay a penalty—six cents.

TR had small feet for a big man, and had to have shoes specially made for him.

TR thought the nation's coins were ugly. So he hired a sculptor named Augustus Saint-Gaudens to design a new penny, nickel, quarter, and half-dollar coin.

TR was the first president to ride in a submarine, and the first to go up in an airplane. When the plane landed, he said, "By George, it was great!"

Woohoo!

TR liked the writing of a poet named Edwin Arlington Robinson. When he heard that Robinson worked for the New York subway because he didn't earn enough money from writing poetry, TR got him a better-paying federal job.

Did you know that Dr. Seuss was really shy?

What does that have to do with TR?

It does, believe me. Dr. Seuss's real name was Theodor Geisel. When he was growing up in Springfield, Massachusetts, he was a Boy Scout. His troop sold war bonds to raise money for the soldiers in World War I. Dr. Seuss sold a lot of them, and the ten boys who sold the most were going to get a medal presented by TR.

But when the ceremony came, there were only nine medals. Dr. Seuss was the tenth kid. The first nine boys got their medals and left the stage. Dr. Seuss was standing there all by himself. Everybody was staring at him. TR shouted, "What's this boy doing here?"

Dr. Seuss was so traumatized that he was

afraid of large crowds for the rest of his life. He hardly ever appeared in public.

Even though they were wealthy, TR and his wife Edith were worried about money when they were younger. Edith made tooth powder from ground-up fish bones and burned alum.

TR's brother Elliott, who was Eleanor Roosevelt's father, was a sad story. As a young man, he became an alcoholic and was sent to an asylum in France. The family tried to have Elliott declared legally insane. After his wife and son died of diphtheria, Elliott tried to jump out a window. He eventually had a seizure and died at the age of thirty-four.

In the *Night at the Museum* movies. Robin Williams played a mannequin of TR that came to life.

All of TR's sons served in the military during World War I. Archie was wounded and almost had his leg amputated. Kermit served in France. Quentin was a pilot and died when his plane was shot down over France. He was just twenty. Theodore Jr. was also wounded, and he won the Distinguished Service Cross and the Silver Star. Like his dad, Theodore was awarded the Medal of Honor. In World War II, he was the only general on D-Day to land by sea with the first wave of troops.

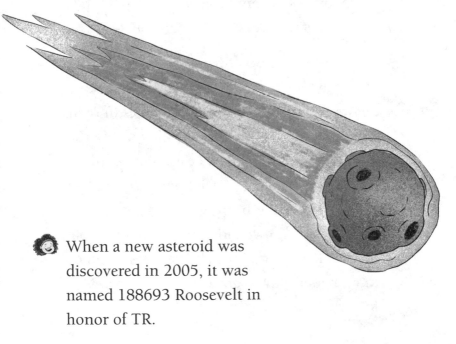

When a new asteroid was discovered in 2005, it was named 188693 Roosevelt in honor of TR.

Hey, look! I think we finished the book!

Yay! This is the last page, so we must be done.

Wait. One more thing. There's something that we forgot to include.

What is it?

Kitty litter!

Oh, I suppose you're going to tell me that somehow TR is connected with kitty litter. Go ahead, let's hear it.

Well, kitty litter was invented in 1947 by a Michigan businessman named Edward Lowe. Before that, people put sand or ashes in their cats' litter boxes. Lowe was selling a type of clay that farmers used as nesting material for chickens. One day his neighbor dropped by and asked if she could borrow some sand for her cat litter box. Lowe didn't have any sand, but he gave her a bag of his clay, and it turned out to be a good way to absorb pee. The rest is history.

So what does the invention of kitty litter have to do with TR?

Nothing. I just thought it was a cool story.

You're impossible.

TO FIND OUT MORE...

Did we get you interested in the life of Teddy Roosevelt? Yay! You can watch dozens of videos about him on YouTube, and there are lots of other books for kids about him too. Ask your librarian if you can't find them.

ACKNOWLEDGMENTS

Thanks to Simon Boughton, Dave Cole, Kristin Allard, Liza Voges, and Nina Wallace. The facts in this book came from many books, videos, web sites, and other sources. Especially helpful was *Theodore Roosevelt: A Life* by Nathan Miller.

ABOUT THE AUTHOR

Dan Gutman has written many books for young readers, such as the My Weird School series, *Houdini and Me*, The Genius Files, Flashback Four, *The Kid Who Ran for President*, *The Homework Machine*, *The Million Dollar Shot*, and his baseball card adventure series. Dan and his wife, Nina, live in New York City. You can find out more about Dan and his books by visiting his website (www.dangutman.com) or following him on Facebook, Twitter, and Instagram.

TITLES IN THE

Wait! WHAT?

SERIES